Vonette Bright's Prayer & Praise Diary

Name_____

Address _____

City _____State_____Zip_____

Phone (_____)_____

Vonette Bright's Prayer & Praise Diary

Great Commission Prayer Crusade
Arrowhead Springs San Bernardino, CA 92414
A ministry of Campus Crusade for Christ International

Scripture references are from the New American Standard Bible unless otherwise identified. Copyright © The Lockman Foundation, 1960, 1962, 1963, 1968, 1971, 1972, 1973. Used by permission.

Scripture quoted from the Living Bible used by permission.

A Campus Crusade for Christ Book
Published by
HERE'S LIFE PUBLISHERS, INC.
P.O. Box 1576
San Bernardino, CA 92402
(714) 886-7981

Product No. 35-06-37
© Copyright 1978, 1981, Campus Crusade for Christ, Inc.

Printed in the United States of America. All rights reserved.

acknowledgments

Grateful thanks and appreciation to Dr. J. Edwin Orr for his kind Introduction and to Dr. Howard Hendricks for his valuable section on "The Family That Prays Together." Also, to Jeannette Hawkinson and the entire Campus Crusade for Christ Prayer Ministry staff for their significant contribution to this Prayer and Praise Diary.

Our prayer is that this diary will become a tool which brings joy to your times of communion with God.

> Vonette Bright and the Staff of the Great Commission Prayer Crusade

contents

- 13 HOW TO USE YOUR PRAYER & PRAISE DAIRY
- 16 HOW TO ENRICH YOUR PRAYER LIFE
- 16 Personal Worship and Interaction
- 20 Personal spiritual development
- 23 Intercession
- 25 Portions of praise
- 29 Portions of promise
- 33 FAMILY PRAYER
- 33 The Family That Prays Together
     by Dr. Howard Hendricks
- 39 SCRIPTURE REFERENCES FOR SPECIFIC PRAYER
- 42 YOUR PRAYER NOTEBOOK
- 42 Daily Personal Prayer Requests
- 51 **Sunday:**
- 51 Worship God – for His holiness
- 52 Prayer for moral & Spiritual awakening
- 52 Personal Prayer List
- 61 **Monday:**
- 61 Worship God – for His sovereignty
- 62 Prayer for National Leaders
- 65 Personal Prayer List
- 73 **Tuesday:**
- 73 Worship God – for His wisdom and knowledge
- 74 Prayer for Local Leaders
- 74 Personal Prayer List
- 85 **Wednesday:**
- 85 Worship God – for His lovingkindness
- 86 Prayer for the Persecuted
- 86 Personal Prayer List
- 93 **Thursday:**
- 93 Worship God – for His power
- 94 Prayer for the Church
- 95 Effective Prayer for the Pastoral Staff
- 96 Personal Prayer List
- 103 **Friday:**
- 103 Worship God – for His righteousness
- 104 Prayer for Christian Impact in Media & Society

- 104 Personal Prayer List
- 111 **Saturday:**
- 111 Worship God—for His faithfulness
- 112 Prayer for Fellow Believers
- 112 Personal Prayer List
- 119 URGENT REQUESTS
- 127 PRAYER FOR THE EVANGELIZATION OF THE WORLD
- 128 Specific World Prayer
- 128 Personal Prayer List
- 136 World Map
- 137 Prayer for the nations
- 140 Prayer for the President
- 141 How to Pray for World Leaders by Jack Hayford

foreword

Even after the disciples of the Lord had walked with Him in person many miles and many months, they came to Him and asked: "Lord, teach us to pray." Did He express great disappointment with them for openly acknowledging their need? No, rather Jesus simply said, "Pray this way...." It has been my privilege to know, in passing, saints of God who certainly excelled in intercession, but I never met a person who seemed satisfied or felt that he or she had now "arrived."

Prayer may sometimes flow from heart and lips just "like a river glorious," but this is usually a rare experience. Prayer is seldom easy, because our human nature is so frail and even more because it represents a warfare against the mighty principalities and powers, the enemy of God. Therefore, any help in stirring up the spirit of prayer or helping its continuance is to be welcomed heartily.

Not all of us are privileged to risk our lives for God in front-line mission work in far-off places, but all of us can participate; nor can we all stand up and preach the gospel to thousands face to face or millions via radio or television, but we can participate. We can comfort lonely folk in hospital or prison, just by prayer. We could probably cite another hundred ways to be involved effectively.

All of us have differing temperaments. Oswald Smith in Canada could hardly bear to be at rest, but made a habit just to walk around a room in prayer, and this is not a bad idea even out of doors provided nothing is permitted to distract. Others must be upon their knees and shut away. Some folks must rise up early to engage in prayer before beginning daily tasks; others need to get the family members off to work or school before discovering a time for quiet prayer and intercession. The main thing is to ascertain the best time of the day for prayer.

No one can develop a prayer life mechanically; yet, on the other hand, everyone who leaves prayer to the impulse of the moment neglects the power of systematic intercession for ever-recurring needs of one and all, personal and worldwide. It is good that the user of this Diary is advised to adjust it to personal needs and times.

This Prayer and Praise Diary, produced by the Great Commission Prayer Crusade, should prove invaluable to those Christians who want their prayer life to count for something in intercessory ministry as well as personal growth in grace. It has an excellent balance of worship of the Almighty with concern for one's own problems and opportunities, as well as the affairs of family, congregation, city, state and nation, the nations of the world and the worldwide church.

When I was 17, I met a missionary who promised me that he would pray for me each day. Occasionally he wrote to me. Then came World War II. I met him once again in London at war's end, found him dying in the Mildmay Hospital. After sharing news and views, I asked him lightly: "Did you keep your word to pray for me each day?" A shadow came across his face. "No, I'm sorry I can't say that." Then he brightened up. "However, I don't think I missed you more than twice, but the pain was very bad those days." I went away ashamed, yet humbly grateful. His name was Ernest Hudson Taylor. How much I owe to prayer!

– J. Edwin Orr

Dear praying friends:

History records no significant movement of the Spirit of God that has not been preceded by a very strong prayer emphasis. And understandably so, because the omnipotent God has chosen to communicate with individuals through prayer as well as through His inspired Word.

Our Savior Himself—to whom all authority in heaven and earth was given—spent much time praying while here on earth. Now seated at the right hand of God the Father, He intercedes on our behalf. Since He is our example, we can rightly conclude that the ministry of prayer is the highest calling a Christian can have.

A vast reservoir of power, wisdom and grace becomes available to us through prayer. God's Word reminds us, "You do not have because you do not ask" (James 4:2). "And everything you ask in prayer, believing, you shall receive" (Matthew 21:22).

The example of our Lord in prayer and the promises of God have encouraged millions of believers to enter into this great adventure of prayer. As a result, the greatest spiritual harvest of all time is taking place throughout the world today.

This prayer and praise diary has been designed and written for the purpose of helping to mobilize and concentrate the prayers of Christians everywhere to accelerate the fulfillment of the Great Commission. It is my earnest prayer that each person who uses this diary will be directed and enabled by the Holy Spirit to become personally involved in praying for a supernatural outpouring of God's Spirit for a worldwide revival.

> Yours for fulfilling the Great Commission in this generation,
> BILL BRIGHT, President and Founder
> Campus Crusade for Christ International

P.S. Study this prayer diary carefully and use it in your daily time of fellowship with the Lord. As you become familiar with the specific prayer requests listed here, you may be reminded of them throughout the day. On these occasions simply respond and pray as the Holy Spirit leads you. As you do, you'll begin to discover the secret of praying "without ceasing."

how to use your prayer & praise diary

The greatest privilege and most revolutionary power available to the Christian is prayer.

By studying the contents of this diary carefully, you will be led through six exciting sections: (1) How to Enrich Your Prayer Life; (2) Family Prayer; (3) Scripture References for Specific Prayer; (4) Your Prayer Notebook; (5) Urgent Prayer Requests; and (6) Prayer for the Evangelization of the World. Section 4 (Your Prayer Notebook) in particular is your day-to-day guide to a powerful ministry of prayer.

God's Word promises us an effective prayer life. "If you abide in Me, and My words abide in you, ask whatever you wish, and it shall be done for you" (John 15:7). "Truly, truly, I say to you, he who believes in Me, the works that I do shall he do also; and greater works than these shall he do; because I go to the Father" (John 14:12).

Never before in the history of man have there been so many questions with so few answers. Most of the problems we face in the world today need spiritual answers. These must come through spiritual people.

The power of united prayer was particularly demonstrated by the early church. In Acts, chapter four, we read that the believers prayed together with one heart, mind and spirit. The Great Commission Prayer Cursade desires to challenge contemporary believers to become people of specific, extraordinary prayer, to assist in establishing united prayer movements in communities and to be instruments in calling Christians of all denominations to pray for a moral and spiritual awakening throughout the world.

You and I have the privilege of calling on God in united, specific prayer to have a part in changing the world, our personal lives and circumstances. We have God's promise that if we who know Him personally are willing to humble ourselves before Him, pray and turn from sins, He will bring the healing influence of His Spirit into our society (II Chronicles 7:14).

Both the Old and New Testaments indicate that when God's people came together to pray specifically, God heard, answered, delivered, empowered and provided all their needs.

It is very difficult to believe God for national and worldwide needs until we have seen Him provide for our personal needs. Faith, like a muscle of the body, needs exercise in order to grow. Since prayer is one way of expressing our faith, in order for prayer to be effective our faith must increase as well. Once we have begun to see answers to our personal prayers, it will become much easier to believe God for answers to prayers concerning our country and the rest of the world.

This prayer diary is designed to enhance your communion with our heavenly Father. Used with one or more of your favorite Bible translations, it will enrich your times of worship, prayer and intercession by providing you with an orderly method of recording your requests, impressions and concerns for yourself, your family, your friends and the world around you.

The following sections suggest different topics for intercession which are being remembered in prayer by thousands of believers around the world on any given day in the week. They will aid you in remembering your prayer requests in an orderly manner. At the same time, they can help make your prayer dynamic and rich through use of the Scriptures as you pray. Add Scripture references as God reveals them to you and adjust the subject as God leads.

The suggested daily subjects may occupy only a few seconds of your daily prayer time, or you may wish to concentrate on one issue, person or event for an extended time. The important point to remember is to name your specific request and to unite with others in prayer for designated subjects (Acts 4:24-32; II Chronicles 20:24).

A permanent and chronological record of God's faithfulness can be kept by noting progress toward prayers being answered and recording dates of answers. This will, in turn, increase your faith in God's limitless love, power and resources.

how to enrich your prayer life

personal worship and interaction

I. Set aside a regular time each day to spend with God, preferably early in the morning. "In the morning, O Lord, Thou wilt hear my voice; in the morning I will order my prayer to Thee and eagerly watch" (Psalm 5:3).

   A. Find a place where you can be alone, free from distractions. "And in the early morning, while it was still dark, He arose and went out and departed to a lonely place, and was praying there" (Mark 1:35).

   B. Take your Bible and your prayer diary in which to record prayers and impressions from God. "Open my eyes, that I may behold wonderful things from Thy law" (Psalm 119:18).

   C. Don't allow intruding thoughts to disrupt your prayer time. Keep a note pad handy to jot down "things to do."

   D. Occasionally include a hymnbook, recorded music or instrument for singing praises unto the Lord. "The Lord is my strength and my shield; my heart trusts in Him, and I am helped; therefore my heart exults, and with my song I shall thank Him" (Psalm 28:7).

   E. Go into God's presence with a spirit of expectance that this time of communion and prayer will reveal God's glory and character to you in a deeper way and that He will meet you at your point of need. "Enter His gates with thanksgiving, and His courts with praise" (Psalm 100:4).

II. Ask God to search your heart. "Search me, O God, and know my heart; try me and know my anxious thoughts; and see if there be any hurtful way in me, and lead me in the everlasting way" (Psalm 139:23,24).

    A. Confess any sins the Holy Spirit reveals. "If I regard wickedness in my heart, the Lord will not hear" (Psalm 66:18). "If we confess our sins, He is faithful and righteous to forgive us our sins and to cleanse us from all unrighteousness" (I John 1:9).

    B. Make certain you are walking and praying in the Spirit. "Therefore be careful how you walk...be filled with the Spirit...always giving thanks for all things in the name of our Lord Jesus Christ to God, even the Father" (Ephesians 5:15,18,20).

III. Wait before the Lord. Listening to God is as important as speaking to God. Allow an unhurried time before God to listen with your heart and mind.

    A. Read passages of Scripture (Psalms, the Old Testament prophets, the epistles, etc.) and pray them back to God, adapting them as worship, praise or requests.

        1. Worship God for who He is. (See Psalms 103 and 104.) Example: "I praise Your holy name with my whole being, Lord...Thank You that my chief benefit is eternal life through Jesus, my Lord...Thank You that His death for me bought my pardon and healed me from the disease of my sin..." (From Psalm 103).

        2. Praise Him for His attributes. (See Psalms 145-150.) Example: "You are eternal and immortal, O God...I praise Your holy name for the privilege of spending eternity in Your presence...The extent of Your greatness surpasses my imagination, Lord. I praise You that You reveal Yourself throughout creation..." (From Psalm 145).

- B. Rejoice in your fellowship with Him, just as He delights in you. "...the prayer of the upright is His delight" (Proverbs 15:8b). (Substitute your name for "the upright.")
- C. Allow unhindered time for God to speak to your heart.

IV. Develop a prayer request list.
- A. Study the 11 characteristics of the Spirit-filled Christian (see the "Personal Spiritual Development" section, following), and ask God to manifest in your life and experience the character traits and responses of Jesus, claiming appropriate Scripture. "But we all, with unveiled face beholding as in a mirror the glory of the Lord, are being transformed into the same image from glory to glory, just as from the Lord, the Spirit" (II Corinthians 3:18).
- B. Use your daily newspaper, periodicals or other news sources to guide you in your prayer for specific individuals and local concerns. Make a list and keep your prayers specific so that you may recognize specific answers as they come.
- C. Pray your way around the world with unhurried, detailed intercession for others.
   - Begin with your non-Christian friends, relatives, neighbors, your pastor and church leadership, missionaries and other believers.
   - Using your newspaper, continue on in prayer for your community, state and country.
   - Pray for those in authority (I Timothy 2:1,2) and any others God may bring to mind. Ask specific requests for them.
   - Pray as Paul prayed for others in Philippians 1, Colossians 1 and Ephesians 1 and 3.
   - Ask for others what you ask for yourself. Desire for them what the Lord has shown you.
- D. Ask for understanding (Psalms 119:18).
  Meditate on Scripture you have memorized or Scripture promises you know.

Read an entire book in the Bible (select one of appropriate length).
1. Ask God to show you personal applications.
2. Pray for yourself. See I Chronicles 4:10.
3. Ask, "Lord, what do **You** think of my life?" Consider your activities: What are your life and ministry objectives? How do you spend your time? Is your time counting for eternity?

Record your thoughts.

Review or plan your use of time for God's greatest glory in various areas of your life: family, work, personal Bible study and devotions, church activities, etc.

Discuss with the Lord problems or decisions you may be facing. Record conclusions God brings to your mind. Look in the Scriptures for promises to claim and underline them.

E. Daily prayer concerns may include one or more of the following:
  - Development of your personal ministry
  - Personal concerns and circumstances
  - Areas of personal influence
  - Family members, their personal desires, development, concerns and circumstances
  - Christian friends
  - Non-believers
  - Those who are discouraged
  - Those who are ill
  - Those in authority over you
  - Upcoming events
  - Selected missionaries and/or missionary outreaches and those who support them
  - Laborers for the harvest fields of the world
  - Revival
  - Moral and spiritual awakening
  - Other.

F. List the date, requests, applicable Scripture, action to be taken, results and date answered, as a record of God's guidance and faithfulness.

personal spiritual development

From the moment that we come to know Jesus Christ personally, we begin the life-long adventure of becoming conformed to the image of Christ. Amazingly enough, God is able to display His own character qualities through His children. He desires us to become men and women who have surrendered to the lordship of Christ and are seeing His character qualities become real in our lives.

The following are the basic character qualities of a Spirit-filled Christian. Use this list as a guide to pray and expect God the Holy Spirit to work these qualities into your life (Philippians 1:6; II Peter 1:3).

1. FAITH: The Spirit-filled Christian is consistently aware of the character of the Triune God, one God manifest in three persons—Father, Son and Holy Spirit. He draws upon the

infinite resources of God by faith in order to live the Christian life. He understands that faith is his response to all that God is and all that He promises to those who trust and obey Him. (Romans 10:17; Galatians 2:20; Philippians 3:7-11; Hebrews 11:6; 12:1,2)

2. STEWARDSHIP: The Spirit-filled Christian allows Christ to be Lord in every area of life—his mind, body, relationships, talents and material possessions. He recognizes that all he has is ultimately a gift of God, and he considers himself a responsible steward of these blessings. (Romans 12:2; I Corinthians 2:16; 6:20; Philippians 4:8; I Peter 4:10; II Peter 1:5-8)

3. POWER: The Spirit-filled Christian allows the Holy Spirit, who indwells him, to increasingly control his daily life. Thus, he is becoming more and more in character like our Lord Jesus Christ. (II Corinthians 12:9,10; Esphesians 3:14-21; Philippians 4:13; Colossians 1:29)

4. PRAYER: Following the example of our Lord, the Disciples and Christian leaders throughout the centuries, the Spirit-filled Christian places a special priority on prayer and his daily communication with God. He realizes that God delights in his fellowship, desires his worship and welcomes his requests. (Matthew 26:41; Acts 5:4; Ephesians 6:18; Philippians 4:4-7; Colossians 4:2)

5. OBEDIENCE: The Spirit-filled Christian seeks to obey God daily. As he understands the commands and desires of God, he is willing to submit to them and make them his own desires. He realizes that obedience to his heavenly Father involves submission to those who are placed in authority over him. (Proverbs 3:5,6; Matthew 26:39; John 4:34; 8:29; Philippians 2:5-8; Hebrews 5:8)

6. DIRECTION: The Spirit-filled Christian depends on the Word of God for direction and guidance in every circumstance. He accepts the Bible as his final authority—his source of knowledge about God, others and himself. (Joshua 1:8,9; Psalm 119:5,6; Matthew 4:4; Colossians 1:9,10; I Thessalonians 5:15; II Timothy 2:15)

7. ACTION: The Spirit-filled Christian views his life as an

opportunity to actively serve his Lord. He is consistently winning others to Christ, helping to build them in their faith and sending them forth as spiritual multipliers to win and build others for the Savior. His purpose is to live for Christ in his own sphere of influence, help to fulfill the Great Commission in his generation and thus help change the world. (Luke 19:10; Acts 26:18; Philippians 1:27; Colossians 1:10; 3:23)

8. LOVE: The Spirit-filled Christian experiences the unconditional, supernatural love of God *(agape)* in his daily life, and expresses that same quality of love in meaningful ways to family, friends and acquaintances — believers and nonbelievers alike. (Luke 10:27; Esphesians 5:1,2; Philippians 1:9-11; I Timothy 1:5; I Peter 4:8)

9. VISION: The Spirit-filled Christian views the world, its problems, needs and opportunities from God's perspective. His prayer is, "Lord Jesus, if You were I, what would You be doing and planning in the power of the Holy Spirit?" He acknowledges that his talents, abilities and dreams are gifts from God and offers them back to the Lord Jesus Christ, trusting Him for their fulfillment. (Psalm 2:8; Luke 19:10; Ephesians 1:18,19; 3:20,21)

10. LEADERSHIP: The Spirit-filled Christian is a leader in the particular area where God has placed him. As such, he consistently encourages others to Christian commitment and Spirit-controlled action, and works to mobilize them in an ongoing movement to help fulfill the Great Commission. (Mark 12:42-44; Luke 6:12,13; Philippians 3:17; I Thessalonians 2:8-12; II Timothy 2:2; I Peter 5:2,3)

11. FELLOWSHIP: The Spirit-filled Christian enjoys fellowship with God's people worldwide. He loves the church, involves himself in it and supports its efforts to fulfill the Great Commission. (II Corinthians 13:11; Ephesians 5:18-21; Philippians 2:1-4; I Thessalonians 2:8-12)

intercession

Our Lord Jesus Christ gave Himself on the cross as intercessor for all men. Intercession is still His unceasing service and ministry to those who draw near to God through Him (Hebrews 7:25).

Next to worship, it is the highest form of service *you* can perform. "The greatest thing anyone can do for God and man is to pray. It is not the only thing, but it is the chief thing" (S.D. Gordon, *Quiet Talks on Prayer*).

"Intercession is the link between man's impotence and God's omnipotence" (Andrew Murray).

An intercessor is one with genuine concern for others, who stands in the gap between man and God making request before God or resisting the devil on man's behalf (Exodus 32:9-14; Psalm 106:23; Ezekiel 22:30,31; James 4:7,8).

As we come to God, we are requesting His hand to be moved on behalf of the person, nation, circumstance and subject of our prayers. The enemy of men's souls is powerless against intercessory prayer.

We are directed by God's Word to intercede for others: "First of all, then, I urge that entreaties and prayers, petitions and thanksgivings, be made on behalf of all men, for kings and all who are in authority, in order that we may lead a tranquil and quiet life in all godliness and dignity. This is good and acceptable in the sight of God our Savior, who desires all men to be saved and to come to the knowledge of the truth" (I Timothy 2:1-4).

A. Empathize with those for whom you are praying.

B. Follow scriptural prayer examples as you intercede. In the majority of Paul's prayers we see him praying specifically for the deepening and development of the spiritual character of those he loves rather than for the circumstances surrounding their lives. (See Ephesians 1:18-20; 3:14-19;

Philippians 1:9-11; Colossians 1:9-12.) Our circumstances are constantly changing but as our character develops, we will be "perfect and complete, lacking nothing" (James 1:4).

Example of adapting Colossians 1:9,10: "Father, please fill George with the knowledge of Your will in all spiritual wisdom and understanding, so that he may walk in a manner worthy of our Lord, to please You in all respects. I pray that George may bear fruit in every good work and increase in the knowledge of You."

C. Pray for the nations of the world. God desires all men to hear the truth of the gospel. "Now bring us back to loving You, O Lord, so that Your anger will never need rise against us again. (Or: will You be always angry—on and on to distant generations?) Oh, revive us! Then Your people can rejoice in You again. Pour out Your love and kindness on us, Lord, and grant us your salvation. I am listening carefully to all the Lord is saying—for He speaks peace to His people, His saints, if they will only stop their sinning. Surely His salvation is near to those who reverence Him; our land will be filled with His glory" (Psalm 85:4-9, Living Bible).

1. Pray that each government will allow Christians within the nation to freely share their faith (Psalm 33:12; Proverbs 14:34).

2. Specifically name those in positions of leadership as you pray (Proverbs 21:1;29:2).

3. Contact your local city hall to obtain names of your city officials.

D. Pray for events and circumstances as well as for individuals. Use your daily newspaper and newscasts as sources for intercessory prayer.

E. Claim the supernatural resources of God to be released in the lives of men and nations separated from God by unbelief and/or ignorance (Ephesians 6:10-20; Colossians 1:13,14). As God's children, we have the responsibility to pray at all times and about all things (Luke 18:1,7).

portions of praise

I Chronicles 16:31,34,36 – "Let the heavens be glad, and let the earth rejoice; and let them say among the nations, 'The Lord reigns.' O give thanks to the Lord, for He is good; for His lovingkindness is everlasting. Blessed be the Lord, the God of Israel from everlasting even to everlasting. Then all the people said, 'Amen,' and praised the Lord."

Psalm 24:7-10 – "Lift up your heads, O gates, and be lifted up, O ancient doors, that the King of glory may come in! Who is the King of glory? The Lord strong and mighty, the Lord mighty in battle. Lift up your heads, O gates, And lift them up, O ancient doors, that the King of glory may come in! Who is this King of glory? The Lord of hosts, He is the King of glory."

Psalm 28:6,7 – "Blessed be the Lord, because He has heard the voice of my supplication. The Lord is my strength and my shield; my heart trusts in Him, and I am helped; therefore my heart exults, and with my song I shall thank Him."

Psalm 30:4 – "Sing praise to the Lord, you His godly ones, and give thanks to His holy name."

Psalm 34:1-3 – "I will bless the Lord at all times; His praise shall continually be in my mouth. My soul shall make its boast in the Lord; the humble shall hear it and rejoice. O magnify the Lord with me, and let us exalt His name together."

Psalm 50:23 – "He who offers a sacrifice of thanksgiving honors Me; and to him who orders his way aright I shall show the salvation of God."

Psalm 56:10-12 – "In God, whose word I praise, in the Lord, whose word I praise, in God I have put my trust. I shall not be afraid. What can man do to me? Thy vows are binding upon me, O God; I will render thank offerings to Thee."

Psalm 63:3-6 – "Because Thy lovingkindness is better than life, my lips will praise Thee. So I will bless Thee as long as I live; I will lift up my hands in Thy name. My soul is satisfied as with marrow and fatness. And my mouth offers praises with joyful lips; when I remember Thee on my bed. I meditate on Thee in the night watches."

Psalm 69:30,34 – "I will praise the name of God with song, and shall magnify Him with thanksgiving. Let heaven and earth praise Him, the seas and everything that moves in them."

Psalm 75:1 – "We give thanks to Thee, O God, we give thanks, for Thy name is near; men declare Thy wondrous works."

Psalm 86:12 – "I will give thanks to Thee, O Lord my God, with all my heart, and will glorify Thy name forever."

Psalm 92:1,2 – "It is good to give thanks to the Lord, and to sing praises to Thy name, O Most High; to declare Thy lovingkindness in the morning, and Thy faithfulness by night."

Isaiah 25:1 – "O Lord, thou art my God; I will exalt Thee, I will give thanks to Thy name; for Thou hast worked wonders, plans formed long ago, with perfect faithfulness."

Isaiah 38:18 – "For Sheol cannot thank Thee, death cannot praise Thee; those who go down to the pit cannot hope for Thy faithfulness."

Daniel 2:20,23 – "Daniel answered and said, 'Let the name of God be blessed forever and ever, for wisdom and power belong to Him. To Thee, O God of my fathers, I give thanks and praise, for Thou hast given me wisdom and power; even now Thou hast made known to me what we requested of Thee, for Thou hast made known to us the king's matter.,"

Acts 2:46,47 – "And day by day continuing with one mind in the temple, and breaking bread from house to house, they were taking their meals together with gladness and sincerity of heart, praising God, and having favor with all the people. And the Lord was adding to their number day by day those who were being saved."

Romans 11:36 – "For from Him and through Him and to Him are all things. To Him be the glory forever. Amen."

I Corinthians 14:15 – "What is the outcome then? I shall pray with the spirit and I shall pray with the mind also; I shall sing with the spirit and I shall sing with the mind also."

I Corinthians 15:57 – "But thanks be to God, who gives us the victory through our Lord Jesus Christ."

Ephesians 1:3 – "Blessed be the God and Father of our Lord Jesus Christ, who has blessed us with every spiritual blessing in the heavenly places in Christ."

Ephesians 5:19 – "Speaking to one another in psalms and hymns and spiritual songs, singing and making melody with your heart to the Lord."

I Timothy 1:17 – "Now to the King eternal, immortal, invisible, the only God, be honor and glory forever and ever. Amen."

Hebrews 13:15 – "Through Him then let us continually offer up a sacrifice of praise to God, that is, the fruit of lips that give thanks to His name."

I Peter 2:9 – "But you are a chosen race, a royal priesthood, a holy nation, a people for God's own possession, that you may proclaim the excellencies of Him who has called you out of darkness into His marvelous light."

I Peter 4:11 – "Whoever speaks, let him speak, as it were, the utterances of God; whoever serves, let him do so as by the strength which God supplies; so that in all things God may be glorified through Jesus Christ, to whom belongs the glory and dominion forever and ever. Amen."

Psalm 103:1 – "Bless the Lord, O my soul; and all that is within me, bless His holy name."

Psalm 104:24,31,33,34 – "O Lord, how many are Thy works! In wisdom Thou has made them all; the earth is full of Thy possessions. Let the glory of the Lord endure forever; let the Lord be glad in His works... I will sing to the Lord as long as I live; I will sing praise to my God while I have my being. Let my meditation be pleasing to Him; as for me, I shall be glad to the Lord."

Psalm 105:2 – "Sing to Him, sing praises to Him; Speak of all His wonders."

Psalm 106:1 – "Praise the Lord! Oh give thanks to the Lord, for He is good; for His lovingkindness is everlasting."

Psalm 107:8,9 – "Let them give thanks to the Lord for His lovingkindness, and for His wonders to the sons of men! For He has satisfied the thirsty soul, and the hungry soul He has filled with what is good."

Psalm 113:3 – "From the rising of the sun to its setting the name of the Lord is to be praised."

Psalm 116:12,17 – "What shall I render to the Lord for all His benefits toward me?...To Thee I shall offer a sacrifice of thanksgiving, and call upon the name of the Lord."

Psalm 118:6 – "The Lord is for me; I will not fear; what can man do to me?"

Psalm 119:62 – "At midnight I shall rise to give thanks to Thee because of Thy righteous ordinances."

Psalm 119:97 – "O how I love Thy law! It is my meditation all the day."

Psalm 119:129 – "Thy testimonies are wonderful; therefore my soul observes them."

portions of promise

"God is not a man, that He should lie..." (Numbers 23:19). "Know therefore that the Lord your God, He is God, the faithful God..." (Deuteronomy 7:9). "...For He who promised is faithful..." (Hebrews 10:23b). "If we are faithless, He remains faithful; for He cannot deny Himself" (II Timothy 2:13). "For as many as may be the promises of God, in Him they are yes; wherefore also by Him is our Amen to the glory of God through us" (II Corinthians 1:20).

Romans 8:26 – "And in the same way the Spirit also helps our weakness; for we do not know how to pray as we should, but the Spirit Himself intercedes for us with groanings too deep for words."

Hebrews 11:6 – "And without faith it is impossible to please Him, for he who comes to God must believe that He is, and that He is a rewarder of those who seek Him."

James 1:5-7 – "But if any of you lacks wisdom, let him ask of God, who gives to all men generously and without reproach, and it will be given to him. But let him ask in faith without any doubting, for the one who doubts is like the surf of the sea driven and tossed by the wind."

James 5:16 – "Therefore, confess your sins to one another, and pray for one another, so that you may be healed. The effective prayer of a righteous man can accomplish much."

I John 5:16 – "And whatever we ask we receive from Him, because we keep His commandments and do the things that are pleasing in His sight."

I John 5:14,15 – "And this is the confidence which we have before Him, that, if we ask anything according to His will, He hears us. And if we know that He hears us in whatever we ask, we know that we have the requests which we have asked from Him."

Psalm 108:13 – "Through God we shall do valiantly; and it is He who will tread down our adversaries."

Psalm 55:1,16,17 – "Give ear to my prayer, O God; and hide not Thyself from my supplication. As for me, I will call upon God; and the Lord shall save me. Evening, and morning, and at noon, will I pray, and cry aloud: and He shall hear my voice" (King James).

Psalm 84:11 – "For Lord God is a sun and shield; the Lord gives grace and glory; no good thing does He withhold from those who walk uprightly."

Psalm 6:9 – "The Lord has heard my supplication, the Lord receives my prayer."

II Chronicles 7:14 – "If...My people who are called by My name humble themselves and pray, and seek My face and turn from their wicked ways, then I will hear from heaven, will forgive their sin, and will heal their land."

Psalm 10:17 – "O Lord, Thou hast heard the desire of the humble; Thou wilt strengthen their heart, Thou wilt incline Thine ear."

Psalm 37:3-5 – "Trust in the Lord, and do good; dwell in the land and cultivate faithfulness. Delight yourself in the Lord; and He will give you the desires of your heart. Commit your way to the Lord, trust also in Him, and He will do it."

Psalm 145:18 – "The Lord is near to all who call upon Him, to all who call upon Him in truth."

Proverbs 3:5,6 – "Trust in the Lord with all your heart, and do not lean on your own understanding. In all your ways acknowlege Him, and He will make your paths straight."

Isaiah 65:24 – "It will also come to pass that before they call, I will answer; and while they are still speaking, I will hear."

Jeremiah 29:12,13 – "Then you will call upon Me and come and pray to Me, and I will listen to you. And you will seek Me and find Me, when you search for Me with all your heart."

Jeremiah 33:3 – "Call to Me, and I will answer you, and I will tell you great and mighty things, which you do not know."

Matthew 7:7,8 – "Ask, and it shall be given to you; seek, and you shall find; knock, and it shall be opened to you. For everyone who asks receives; and he who seeks finds; and to him who knocks it shall be opened."

Matthew 18:19,20 – "Again I say to you, that if two of you agree on earth about anything that they may ask, it shall be done for them by My Father who is in heaven. For where two or three have gathered together in My name, there I am in their midst."

Matthew 21:22 – "And everything you ask in prayer, believing, you shall receive."

Luke 11:13 – "If you then, being evil, know how to give good gifts to your children, how much more shall your Heavenly Father give the Holy Spirit to those who ask Him?"

John 14:13,14 – "And whatever you ask in My name, that will I do, that the Father may be glorified in the Son. If you ask Me anything in My name, I will do it."

Romans 8:28,32 – "And we know that God causes all things to work together for good to those who love God, to those who are called according to His purpose...He who did not spare His own Son, but delivered Him up for us all, how will He not also with Him freely give us all things?"

I Peter 5:7 – "Casting all your anxiety upon Him, because He cares for you."

Psalm 55:22 – "Cast your burden upon the Lord, and He will sustain you; He will never allow the righteous to be shaken."

Isaiah 41:10 – "Do not fear, for I am with you; do not anxiously look about you, for I am your God. I will strengthen you, surely I will help you, surely, I will uphold you with My righteous right hand."

Philippians 4:19 – "And my God shall supply all your needs according to His riches in glory in Christ Jesus."

Matthew 6:33 – "But seek first His kingdom, and His righteousness; and all these things shall be added to you."

Proverbs 16:1 – "The plans of the heart belong to man, but the answer of the tongue is from the Lord."

Zechariah 13:9b – "They will call on My name, and I will answer them; I will say, 'They are My people,' and they will say, 'The Lord is my God.'"

Mark 11:22-24 – "And Jesus answered saying to them, 'Have faith in God. Truly I say to you, whoever says to this mountain,

"Be taken up and cast into the sea," and does not doubt in his heart, but believes that what he says is going to happen; it shall be granted him. Therefore I say to you, all things for which you pray and ask, believe that you have received them, and they shall be granted to you.'"

John 9:31 – "We know that God does not hear sinners; but if any one is God-fearing, and does His will, He hears him."

John 15:7,16 – "If you abide in Me, and My words abide in you, ask whatever you wish, and it shall be done for you. You did not choose Me, but I chose you, and appointed you, that you should go and bear fruit, and that your fruit should remain; that whatever you ask of the Father in My name, He may give to you."

John 16:23b,24 – "...I say to you, if you shall ask the Father for anything, He will give it to you in My name. Until now you have asked for nothing in My name; ask, and you will receive, that your joy may be made full."

Ephesians 3:20,21 – "Now to Him who is able to do exceeding abundantly beyond all that we ask or think, according to the power that works within us, to Him be the glory in the church and in Christ Jesus to all generations forever and ever. Amen."

I Thessalonians 5:17,18 – "Pray without ceasing; in everything give thanks; for this is God's will for you in Christ Jesus."

Hebrews 10:22,23b – "Let us draw near with a sincere heart in full assurance of faith, having our hearts sprinkled clean from an evil conscience and our body washed with pure water...for He who promised is faithful."

family prayer

the family that prays together
Dr. Howard Hendricks

We are living in a generation whose homes are falling apart at the seams. They are falling apart not because they have problems, but because they have no prayer. The family that prays together does so as a result of three convictions.

Prayer Is Caught
First of all, the family that prays together has the conviction that prayer must be caught.

Very early in the game the Savior could have said to His men, "Now gentlemen, if we are going to reach the world for Christ, you must be infected with the basics. So the first thing I want to teach you is the paramount importance of prayer." He could have said that, but He did not. Instead, He spent nights in prayer. In fact, every time the disciples looked for Him, they found Him on His knees. Until finally, a long way down the line, they said, "Lord, teach us to pray." Would the members of your family ever find you on your knees so frequently that they would be compelled to say, "Mom, Dad, teach us to pray"?

One day I asked one of my seminary students, "What do you remember most about your father?"

He said, "Prof, I remember that I used to have a paper route in the morning, and I had to get up very early. I'd go by my parents' bedroom at 4 in the morning and I would look in and see my father on his knees. I was profoundly impressed, but as a child I said to myself, 'There's nobody listening. He's certainly not trying to impress anybody.' Finally it dawned on me—his relationship with the living Lord was very real. The second thing I remember is my father rolling on the floor, laughing with us kids."

I thought to myself, what an invincible combination—a father on his knees in prayer, and on the floor laughing with his kids.

The members of your family are looking to you to model the importance of prayer. Prayer is the recognition that our need is not partial; it is total. The Christian life is not difficult; it is impossible. It is a supernatural life and until we learn to tap supernatural resources we can never set an adequate example for others in the faith. Our children are looking for us to convince them by our actions that we are parents dependent on God.

Prayer Is Taught

Second, a family that is committed to prayer is convinced not only that prayer is caught, but that prayer must be taught. Note the order: It is better caught before it is taught. You cannot impart what you do not possess. If you do not have the disease, you cannot spread it. Isaiah said, "A father tells his sons about Thy faithfulness." Moses said, "These words...shall be on your heart; and you shall teach them diligently to your sons" (Deuteronomy 6:6-7). May I suggest four components of prayer that we need to teach our children?

First, we need to teach the members of our family that prayer involves **petition**. Petition is not a process of twisting God's reluctant arm, asking Him to do something that He really would rather not do, thinking that if we make ourselves obnoxious enough, He may come through. Prayer is not an Aladdin's lamp that you rub and get your wish. Prayer is the process of seeking the will of God in one's life. Therefore, we ought to be very specific in teaching our children to pray for needs in every area—in the physical area, in the social area, in the intellectual area and in the spiritual area.

In addition to petition, there is **thanksgiving**. Paul said, "In everything give thanks" (Thessalonians 5:18). So often we spend all our time asking God for things. In the process, we give our children a distorted impression of prayer. Prayer becomes to them like Old MacDonald's farm, with a "gimme, gimme here, and a gimme, gimme there; here a gimme, there a gimme, everywhere a gimme, gimme."

Also, there is the component of **adoration** or worship. Study the prayers of both Old and New Testaments and you will find again and again that wherever people turn to God in prayer, they remind themselves who God is. And because God is the kind of Person that He is, I know that He can meet my needs.

I gave a student an assignment one day. I said, "I want you to go back to your room and I want you to pray for five minutes without asking God for one thing." When I saw him later on campus, he said, "Prof, I got down on my knees. I brought everything I could think of to God. I got up and looked at my watch. Three minutes had passed."

A fourth component is **intercession**, praying for others, both within the family and without—for the government, for people who are in positions of authority, for our neighbors, our children's playmates, the church and the world. Your children will grow up convinced that your perspective is a world perspective if that is what your prayer life is.

Prayer Is Bought
Finally, prayer must not only be caught and taught; it must also be bought. Too much Christian experience in Christian homes is second-hand. We exhort our children to pray but we do not provide an example and an experience with the reality of prayer.

This is why God allows problems to come into our homes. C.S. Lewis said, "Problems are God's megaphones to get our attention." And so He brings crisis and disappointments and all kinds of hassles into human experience to drive you to your knees. I am convinced that is why God allows some parents not only to hit the floor but to break clean through—so that in their anguish they cry out, "Oh God, unless You do something, nothing will be done." He loves to hear that because then, when He meets your needs, you will never be able to say, "I was an adequate parent." All you will be able to say is "To God be the glory. Great things He hath done."

Socrates once said, "Generalities are a refuge for a weak mind." I believe generalities in prayer are a refuge for a weak spiritual commitment. Years ago my wife and I got ourselves a little loose leaf notebook. We opened it flat and on one side we wrote, "We asked," and on the other side we wrote, "He answered." I would not substitute anything for what this notebook did to teach my children the theology of prayer. Nothing is as exciting as writing down a specific request.

When I first started teaching at the seminary, we were several months behind in our salary. I was down to the last meal. I went to my family and I said, "Kids, let's ask Jesus for $10." And we wrote down $10 in that little prayer request notebook.

I went down to the seminary, taught a couple of classes and dropped by the post office. There I found a letter from a friend of mine I had not heard from for years. He wrote, "Howie, I just got a copy of the seminary bulletin. I see you're teaching at the seminary. My wife and I were asking God last night where we could send some of our money, and we felt compelled to send it to you. If you don't need it, pass it on to someone else." I turned over the back page and there, beneath a paper clip, was a $10 bill.

I can still remember bringing that home and saying, "Look at this, kids. Isn't this fantastic?" My older daughter said, "What's so fantastic about that? Isn't that what we asked Jesus for?" And I crawled under a rug.

Sometimes we put requests there and God says, "No." And we thank God for that. We are related to a good heavenly Father, and just like good earthly fathers, He does not give His children everything they ask for.

Nothing is sliced so real as life in the home. The home provides an opportunity to teach children the most significant experiences in all of life.

Years ago when my children were very small, I had a scholar in my home. I knew he was a scholar because he told me so three times. His visit happened to overlap our family worship time, so we invited him to participate. My kids thanked Jesus for the sand pile and the tricycle and the fence, and this man could scarcely wait to get me in the living room. He said, "Professor Hendricks, you don't mean to tell me that you teach in a theological seminary and you teach your children to pray for things like that, do you?"

I said, "Certainly. Did you ever pray about your Ford?"

"Sure." I knew he did; he was riding mostly on faith and fabric.

I said, "Whatever made you think your Ford was more important to God than my boy's tricycle? Did you ever pray for protection?"

"Professor, I never get into my car without praying about the hazards of the highway."

"Well," I said, "that's what my son is praying for when he thanks Jesus for that fence. It keeps out those great big dogs on the other side."

Most of us are educated beyond our intelligence. It's a good thing to return periodically to the place where you learn to pray from your children. Jesus said, "Unless you...become like children, you shall not enter the kingdom of heaven" (Matthew 18:3). Childishness—that is always deplored. Childlikeness—that is always the example.

One of the most critical verses in the New Testament is found in the Gospel of Mark, where we read, "And in the early morning, while it was still dark, He arose and went out and departed to a lonely place, and was praying there" (Mark 1:35). What morning? Why, the morning after the busiest recorded day in the life of our Lord. It had been a day crowded with the performance of miracles, teaching and exposure to people. No one except the persons who have sustained a public ministry have any idea how that can drain an individual. But so high on His priority list was intercourse with the infinite God that the next morning, a great while before day, He retreated to a solitary place to pray.

How to develop habits of family prayer.

Take turns saying grace at mealtime.

As a husband and wife, take one or two minutes in the morning together to pray for each other's daily schedule.

Pray for your children as they leave for school.

Spend five minutes or more in family conversational prayer before the children go to bed.

As husband and wife, end the day praying together over family and personal concerns.

Prayer Handbook - Volume I

scripture references for specific prayer

YOURSELF: Pray for purification of your thoughts and deeds—that you may be a fit instrument and channel for God's love where you live, work, worship and play.

I Corinthians 1:26-31
II Corinthians 2:14,15
Philippians 4:8
Colossians 1:9-12
Peter 1:13-16; 5:6

YOUR HOME AND FAMILY: Pray for a Christ-centered home and family. Seek God's wisdom and guidance in applying His principles.

Psalm 1:1-3; 16:11; 37:23,24; 127:1a
Proverbs 3:33
Ephesians 3:13-19; 4:31,32; 5:1-4,22-6:4
I Peter 3:8,9

THE CONGREGATION: Pray that, as individuals, we will realize God's love and draw upon His wisdom and understanding.

Psalm 1:1-3; 16:11; 37:23,24   Ephesians 3:13-19; 5:1-4

THE CHURCH: Pray for the church and church-related organizations—for unity within the body of Christ.

John 17:11
Acts 1:14; 2:42
I Corinthians 12:12,13
Ephesians 4:1-3,11-16
Philippians 2:1-7

THE COMMUNITY: Pray that Christians in your community will become vital witnesses for Christ through their lives and words.

Psalm 127:1b
Jeremiah 33:3-8
I Corinthians 10:24
II Corinthians 2:14-17; 5:14-21

THE NATION: Pray for national repentance, acknowledging God's mercy and forgiveness (II Chronicles 7:14). Throughout history there seem to have been various crises which threatened the well-being of a nation and demanded specific, united prayer.

In each case, united prayer brought dramatic, powerful intervention by God on their behalf.

II Chronicles 13:12; 15:2; 20:3-6,12; 24:20; 30:12
Ezra 8:21-23
Ezekiel 8:17,18

THE WORLD: Pray for a spirit of revival to sweep the world, that the nations of the world will worship the Lord with reverence.

Psalm 2
Psalm 33:8,10-12

THOSE IN AUTHORITY: Pray for our leaders—local, state and national—that they may have wisdom, integrity, protection, guidance and an awareness of God's presence in mind and heart.

I Samuel 12:14,15
Jeremiah 33:3
Romans 13:1
I Corinthians 2:5
I Timothy 1:6; 2:1-6

THOSE WHO ARE NON-BELIEVERS: Pray for the evangelization of our country and of the world. Pray for the lost to be freed from the enemy, enlightened through the gospel, granted repentance and drawn by the Father.

Matthew 9:27,38
John 6:44; 14:13,14
Romans 10:1,13-15
II Corinthians 4:3,4
Ephesians 2:2
I Timothy 2:4-6
II Timothy 2:25,26
II Peter 3:9
Revelation 3:20

THE SICK, DISCOURAGED AND PERSECUTED: Pray for God's mercy, strength and lovingkindness for those in distress. Pray that they may claim His promises and be aware of His presence. Pray that non-Christians will come to know Christ personally as a result of these trials.

Psalm 118:5,6; 121:2
Matthew 4:23,24
Acts 3:16,19
II Corinthians 1:3,4; 4:16,17; 12:8-10
Ephesians 5:20
Philippians 2:27
James 5:14,15
I Peter 5:7

PRISONERS: Pray for those imprisoned for crimes, and those who are prisoners of alcohol and drugs, immorality, obscenity, pornography, prejudice, unbelief and despair.

Psalm 146:7b Romans 6:19-23
Matthew 5:44-45 I Corinthians 10:13
John 8:31,32,36 II Corinthians 3:17

MASS MEDIA: Pray for a greater Christian influence in newspapers, magazines, television and movies.

Proverbs 1:7; 2:22; 15:26,28,31 Colossians 2:8

your prayer notebook

"...He has granted to us His precious and magnificent promises, in order that by them you might become partakers of the divine nature..." II Peter 1:4.

You can claim God's precious promises daily as you pray for the development of your personal maturity. Evaluate your personal spiritual development by studying the characteristics of the Spirit-filled Christian (see previous section, "Personal Spiritual Development"). List your strengths and weaknesses. Ask God to increase your strengths and overcome your weaknesses. Then believe and receive His provision.

Your daily prayer requests should be recorded on pages in this section.

daily personal prayer requests

Personal Daily

Date	Request	Scripture	Update/Answer Date

Date	Request	Scripture	Update/Answer Date

Date	Request	Scripture	Update/Answer Date

Date	Request	Scripture	Update/Answer Date

Date	Request	Scripture	Update/Answer Date

Date	Request	Scripture	Update/Answer Date

Date	Request	Scripture	Update/Answer Date

Date	Request	Scripture	Update/Answer Date

sunday

worship God for His holiness and immutability

Holy, holy, holy are You, Lord of Hosts. The whole earth is full of Your glory. You are the high and exalted One who lives forever and whose name is Holy. You are enthroned upon the praises of Your people. Your testimonies are fully confirmed and holiness befits Your house, O Lord, forevermore. You are light and in You is no darkness nor variation.

Holy, holy, holy are You, Lord God almighty, who was and who is and who is to come. Who will not fear You, O Lord, and glorify Your name? For You alone are Holy. (From Isaiah 6:3; 57:15; Psalms 22:3, 93:5; I John 1:5; James 1:17; Revelation 4:8; 15:4)

Your godly ones sing praises to You, Lord, and give thanks to Your holy name. You hate all who do iniquity. You have said, "You shall be Holy, for I am Holy." You have not called us for the purpose of impurity, but in sanctification, and You discipline us for our good, so that we may share in Your holiness. We exalt You, O Lord, our God, and worship at Your footstool. (From Psalms 30:4; 5:5a; I Peter 1:16; I Thessalonians 4:7; Hebrews 12:10; Psalm 99:5)

"...I am the Lord, I change not" (Malachi 3:6, King James Version).

"Forever, O Lord, Thy word is settled in heaven. Thy faithfulness continues throughout all generations; Thou didst establish the earth, and it stands" (Psalm 119:89,90).

"Thou, Lord, in the beginning didst lay the foundation of the earth, and the heavens are the works of Thy hands; they will perish, but Thou remainest; and they all will become old as a garment, and as a mantle Thou wilt roll them up; as a garment they will also be changed. But Thou art the same, and Thy years will not come to an end" (Hebrews 1:10-12).

pray for moral and spiritual awakening in the world

Pray for a moral and spiritual awakening in the entire world, acknowledging God's mercy and forgiveness.

"If...My people who are called by My name humble themselves and pray, and seek My face and turn from their wicked ways, then I will hear from heaven, will forgive their sins, and will heal their land" (II Chronicles 7:14).
Pray for:

- Personal renewal and confession of all known sin (Psalm 66:18; I John 1:9).

- Individual Christians – that they might realize God's love and draw upon His moral character and understanding (Psalms 1:1-3; 16:11; 37:23,24; Proverbs 3:5,6; Ephesians 3:13-19; 5:1-4; James 1:5).

- Youth and their families, that they may desire to listen to and learn from each other (Psalm 127:1a; Proverbs 3:33; Ephesians 4:31,32; 5:22-6:4; Colossians 1:10; I Peter 3:8,9).

- Christians to become vital witnesses for Christ through their lives and words (II Corinthians 5:17-20).

- Christians to meet the conditions for revival set forth in II Chronicles 7:14:

    1. Humble themselves (I Peter 5:6).

    2. Pray effectually (James 5:16; Luke 18:1).

    3. Seek God's face (Jeremiah 29:13).

    4. Turn from their wicked ways (I John 1:8,9).

    Other requests:

Date	Request	Scripture	Update/Answer Date

Date	Request	Scripture	Update/Answer Date

Date	Request	Scripture	Update/Answer Date

Date	Request	Scripture	Update/Answer Date

Date	Request	Scripture	Update/Answer Date

Date	Request	Scripture	Update/Answer Date

Date	Request	Scripture	Update/Answer Date

Date	Request	Scripture	Update/Answer Date

monday

worship God
for His sovereignty

You are God and there is no other; You are God and there is no one like You, declaring the end from the beginning. Your purpose will be established and You will accomplish all Your good pleasure. Whatever You please, Lord, You do, in heaven and in earth and in the seas and all the deeps. (From Isaiah 46:9,10; Psalm 135:6)

O Lord God, all the inhabitants of earth are accounted as nothing, but You do according to Your will in the host of heaven and among the inhabitants of earth; and no one can ward off Your hand or say to You, "What have You done?" (From Daniel 4:35)

The heavens will praise Your wonders, O Lord; Your faithfulness also in the assembly of the holy ones. For who in the skies is comparable to You, Lord? Who among the sons of the mighty is like You? You are a God greatly to be feared in the council of the holy ones, and awesome above all those who are around You. O Lord God of hosts, who is like You, O mighty Lord? You work all things after the counsel of Your will. Everything You do will remain forever; there is nothing to add to it and there is nothing to take from it. (From Psalm 89:5-8; Ephesians 1:11; Ecclesiastes 3:14)

Behold, the nations are like a drop from a bucket to You, O Lord, and are regarded as a speck of dust on the scales. Behold, You lift up the islands like fine dust. All the nations are as nothing before You, they are regarded by You as less than nothing and meaningless. You sit above the vault of the earth, and its inhabitants are like grasshoppers. You reduce rulers to nothing and make judges of the earth meaningless. (From Isaiah 40:15,17,22,23)

"...It is He who changes the times and the epochs; He removes kings and establishes kings; He gives wisdom to wise men and knowledge to men of understanding" (Daniel 2:21)

prayer for national leaders

Pray for the leaders of your country by name — that they might have protection, guidance, wisdom, and awareness of God's presence in mind and heart and that they might practice integrity (I Samuel 12:14; I Timothy 2:1-6).

>Head of government
>Governmental officials
>Congressional (parliamentary) representatives
>Governmental advisers
>Members of the judicial system
>Military officers
>Ambassadors and others in places of authority at home and abroad

Pray that:

- They might trust in God with all their heart and not lean on their own understanding; that they will acknowledge Him in all their ways (Proverbs 3:5,6).
- They will seek to have a conscience void of offense toward God and men (Acts 24:16).
- God will place men and women of righteousness, such as Joseph, Daniel, Nehemiah and Mordecai, in positions of authority to lead the nations in righteousness (Proverbs 14:34; 16:12).
- Legislation in your country will be in line with principles from the Word of God.
- Our nation will once again exalt righteousness (Psalm 33:12).
- Righteousness will be the new standard throughout the United States (Proverbs 11:11).
- Christians will be aware of governmental issues, will support leaders in prayer and act regarding issues concerning the moral and spiritual climate of the country.
- God will send a great spiritual awakening to America, that many millions of citizens will receive Christ as Savior and Lord and that Christians will dedicate themselves to God for spiritual living and active service in family, church and national matters.

For U.S.A.
Use appropriate titles for your country

(Write in Names)

President _____

Vice President _____

Cabinet Members

Secretary of State _____

Secretary of the Treasury _____

Secretary of Defense _____

Secretary of the Interior _____

Secretary of Agriculture _____

Secretary of Commerce _____

Secretary of Labor _____

Secretary of Health and Human Services _____

Secretary of Education _____

Secretary of Housing and Urban Development _____

Secretary of Transportation _____

Attorney General _____

Secretary of Energy _____

Supreme Court Justices

Chief Justice Warren E. Burger
Justice William J. Brennan, Jr.
Justice Byron R. White
Justice Thurgood Marshall
Justice Harry A. Blackmun
Justice Lewis F. Powell, Jr.
Justice William H. Rehnquist
Justice John Paul Stevens

Our Senators

_____

_____

Our Congressmen

_____

_____

_____

_____

_____

Elected Officials of Your Country

_____

_____

_____

_____

Date	Request	Scripture	Update/Answer Date

Date	Request	Scripture	Update/Answer Date

Date	Request	Scripture	Update/Answer Date

Date	Request	Scripture	Update/Answer Date

Date	Request	Scripture	Update/Answer Date

Date	Request	Scripture	Update/Answer Date

Date	Request	Scripture	Update/Answer Date

Date	Request	Scripture	Update/Answer Date

tuesday

worship God for His wisdom and knowledge

"Oh the depth of the riches both of the wisdom and knowledge of God! How unsearchable are His judgments and unfathomable His ways! For who has known the mind of the Lord, or who became His counselor? Or who has first given to Him that it might be paid back to Him again? For from Him and through Him and to Him are all things. To Him be the glory forever. Amen" (Romans 11:33-36).

"Wisdom without power would be pathetic, a broken reed; power without wisdom would be merely frightening; but in God boundless wisdom and endless power are united, and this makes Him utterly worthy of our fullest trust" (J.I. Packer, *Knowing God*, p. 81).

"...Let the name of God be blessed forever and ever, for wisdom and power belong to Him" (Daniel 2:20).

O gracious Lord, by wisdom You founded the earth, by understanding You established the heavens. We will lift up our eyes on high and see who has created the stars, the one who leads forth their host by number and calls them all by name. Because of the greatness of Your might and the strength of Your power, not one of them is missing. You are the everlasting God, the Lord, the creator of the ends of the earth who does not become weary or tired. Your understanding is inscrutable. (From Proverbs 3:19; Isaiah 40:26,28)

O Lord, how many are Your works! In wisdom You have made them all. There is no creature hidden from Your sight, but all things are open and laid bare before Your eyes. You know our frame and are mindful that we are but dust. You have placed our iniquities and our secret sins in the light of Your presence. (From Psalm 104:24; Hebrews 4:13; Psalms 103:14; 90:8)

See also Psalm 139.

prayer for local leaders

Pray for leaders of your state or province, county, district and city (Psalm 127:1; Romans 13:1-5).

Governor	Courts
Lieutenant Governor	District administrators
Legislators	Mayor and other city officials
Provincial administrators	Law enforcement
County officials	Public and private school authorities

Pray that:
- God will give Christian leaders knowledge and discernment so that they may be able to distinguish between right and wrong (Philippians 1:9,10).
- God will expose unrighteousness in high places. Ask that He will grant repentance to unbelievers leading to a knowldge of the truth, and that those who are sensitive to His Spirit will remain in their positions of authority (Proverbs 10:9; Daniel 2:21; John 16:31; II Timothy 2:25).
- Our leadership would embody godly character and hate the things God hates:
  "haughty eyes, a lying tongue, hands that shed innocent blood, a heart that devises wicked plans, feet that run rapidly to evil, a false witness who utters lies, and one who spreads strife among brothers" (Proverbs 6:16-19).
- "The wicked will not rule the godly, lest the godly be forced to do wrong" (Psalm 125:3 Living Bible). Pray that God's plan for the rule of the righteous will become an ever-present reality in our generation. "With good men in authority, the people rejoice, but with the wicked in power, they groan" (Proverbs 29:2 Living Bible).

Other requests:

(Use names and titles appropriate to your locality.)
State Government

Governor
___

Lieutenant
  Governor
___

Secretary of
  State
___

Attorney
  General
___

State Representative
  or Assemblyman
___

Local Government

Mayor of
  the city
___

Commissioners
  of the city
___

President of Board
  of Commissioners
___

District
  Attorney
___

City Attorney
City Counsel
___

Councilmen
___

Aldermen
___

Court Officials

Presiding Justice _____

Judges _____

Clerks _____

Education Officials

President of
   college or university _____

Professors _____

Superintendent
   of Schools _____

Members of Board
   of Education _____

Principals _____

Teachers _____

Others

Chief of Police _____

Fire Chief _____

Date	Request	Scripture	Update/Answer Date

Date	Request	Scripture	Update/Answer Date

Date	Request	Scripture	Update/Answer Date

Date	Request	Scripture	Update/Answer Date

Date	Request	Scripture	Update/Answer Date

Date	Request	Scripture	Update/Answer Date

Date	Request	Scripture	Update/Answer Date

Date	Request	Scripture	Update/Answer Date

wednesday

worship God for His lovingkindness

Your lovingkindness endures all day long, O God. You love righteousness and justice, and the earth is full of Your lovingkindness. I will give thanks to You, O Lord, for You are good and ready to forgive and abundant in lovingkindness to all who call upon You. (From Psalms 52:1; 51:1, 33:5; 136:1; 86:5)

As high as the heavens are above the earth, O Lord, so great is Your lovingkindness toward those who fear You. Your lovingkindness is from everlasting to everlasting on those who fear You, for You are gracious and merciful, slow to anger and great in lovingkindness. (From Psalms 103:11,17; 145:8)

"Thy lovingkindness, O Lord, extends to the heavens, Thy faithfulness reaches to the skies. Thy righteousness is like the mountains of God; Thy judgments are like a great deep. O Lord, Thou preservest man and beast. How precious is Thy lovingkindness, O God! And the children of men take refuge in the shadow of Thy wings. They drink their fill of abundance of Thy house; and Thou dost give them to drink of the river of Thy delights. For with Thee is the fountain of life; in Thy light we see light" (Psalm 36:5-9).

Yes, I shall joyfully sing of Your lovingkindness in the morning. (From Psalm 59:16)

"'...but let him who boasts boast of this, that he understands and knows Me, that I am the Lord who exercises lovingkindness, justice and righteousness on earth; for I delight in these things', declares the Lord" (Jeremiah 9:24).

"O satisfy us in the morning with Thy lovingkindness, that we may sing for joy and be glad all our days" (Psalm 90:14).

See also Psalms 23:6; 103:8; 107:43; Proverbs 16:6; Lamentations 3:31,32.

pray for the persecuted

Pray for those undergoing persecution, imprisonment or privation.

Pray for:

- All persons being persecuted for their commitment to Christ around the world (Psalm 91:14-16).
- Prisoners of drugs, alcohol, immorality, obscenity, pornography, crime, prejudice, unbelief and despair (Matthew 5:44,45; John 8:31,21,26; Romans 6:19-23; I Corinthians 10:13; II Corinthians 3:17).
- Prisoners of poverty and hunger (I Samuel 2:8; Job 5:15,16; Psalms 34:10; 50:14,15; 69:33; 72:12,13; 107:41; 140:12; 146:7; Philippians 4:19).

Other requests:

Date	Request	Scripture	Update/Answer Date

Date	Request	Scripture	Update/Answer Date

Date	Request	Scripture	Update/Answer Date

Date	Request	Scripture	Update/Answer Date

Date	Request	Scripture	Update/Answer Date

Date	Request	Scripture	Update/Answer Date

thursday

worship God for His power

Yours, O Lord, is the greatness and the power and the glory and the victory and the majesty, indeed, everything that is in the heavens and the earth. Yours is the dominion, O Lord, and You exalt Yourself as head over all. Both riches and honor come from You, and You rule over all, and in Your hand is power and might; and it lies in Your hand to make great and to strengthen everyone. Now therefore, our God, we thank You and praise Your glorious name. (From I Chronicles 29:11-13)

You ask, "Where were you when I laid the foundation of the earth! Tell Me, if you have understanding." By Your word, O Lord, the heavens were made and by the breath of Your mouth all their host. You uphold all things by the word of Your power. You are the Mighty One, O God; You have spoken, and summoned the earth from the rising of the sun to its setting. Who is like You, majestic in holiness, awesome in praises, working wonders? (From Job 38:4; Psalm 33:6; Hebrews 1:3; Psalm 50:1; Exodus 15:11)

You are the blessed and only sovereign, the King of kings and Lord of lords. You alone possess immortality and dwell in unapproachable light; whom no man has seen or can see. To You are honor and eternal dominion. O Lord, the God of our Fathers, are You not ruler over all the kingdoms of the nations? Power and might are in Your hand so that no one can stand against You. (From I Timothy 6:15,16; II Chronicles 20:6)

Great are You, O Lord, and abundant in strength; Your understanding is infinite. Your eyes are in every place, watching the evil and the good. There is no wisdom and no understanding and no counsel against You, Lord; You are a righteous judge and a God who has indignation every day. (From Psalms 147:5; 34:15,16; Proverbs 21:30; Psalm 7:11)

"Once God has spoken; twice I have heard this: that power belongs to God" (Psalm 62:11).

"The Lord is slow to anger and great in power..." (Nahum 1:3a).

prayer for the Church

Pray for the Church and for church-related organizations, locally and worldwide.

Pray for:

- Unity within the body of Christ and for the evangelization of the world (John 17:11; Acts 4:29,32; I Timothy 2:4).

Ministers	Theological schools	Teachers
Deacons and elders	Missionaries	Evangelists
Laymen	Chaplains	Strategic events

- God's servants to walk in a manner worthy of the calling with which they have been called, with all humility and gentleness, with patience, showing forbearance to one another in love, being diligent to preserve the unity of the Spirit in the bond of peace (Ephesians 4:1-3).
- Each messenger of God—that utterance may be given in the opening of his mouth to make known with boldness the mystery of the gospel (Ephesians 6:19; Colossians 4:3,4).
- God's men and women to be devoted to prayer (Acts 1:14; 2:42; Ephesians 6:18; Colossians 4:2; I Thessalonians 5:16-22).
- His servants to cleanse themselves from all defilement of flesh and spirit, and live in the fear of God (II Corinthians 7:1).
- Good stewardship of resources and the proper commitment of all financial needs to God.
- God's people to learn to engage in good deeds to meet pressing needs, that they may not be unfruitful (Titus 3:14).
- Pastors worldwide to make (as a) high priority the "...equipping of the saints for the work of service, to the building up of the body of Christ" (Ephesians 4:12).
- Pastors to "be diligent to present (themselves) approved to God as (workmen) who do not need to be ashamed, handling accurately the word of truth (II Timothy 2:15).
- The pulpits of America's churches to be aflame with righteousness and that this flame will spread throughout the world.
- Decisions on all levels of government that will enhance the growth of the church and the spread of the gospel worldwide.

effective prayer for the pastoral staff

Pray for:

Each staff member's relationship to God. Pray that they will
- Be Spirit-filled servants of God (Ephesians 3:14-16).
- Grow in their knowledge and walk (Ephesians 1:16-19).
- Be protected from the evil one (II Thessalonians 3:1-3; Ephesians 6:12,13).
- Have discernment and love for others (Colossians 1:9-11).
- Keep their thoughts on Christ (Philippians 4:8).
- Continue to grow in their prayer life (Colossians 4:2).

Each staff member's relationship to his family. Pray that
- Each will spend quality time with his children (Deuteronomy 6:6-10).
- Each man will become the husband described in Ephesians 5:25-33.
- Each woman will become like the wife described in Proverbs 31.
- His children might walk in the ways of the Lord (Psalm 78:5-7).

Each staff member's relationship to his ministry. Pray that
- He will preach the Word in a clear and effective manner (Colossians 4:3,5; Ephesians 6:19,20).
- Revival would take hold in the church body (Psalm 85:6).
- Pastors would be able to train faithful men to disciple the flock (II Timothy 2:2; Ephesians 4:11).
- Unity might continue to grow in the church (John 17:21).
- God will make opportunities to share Christ this week (Colossians 4:5,6; I Peter 3:15; II Corinthians 5:17-20).

Date	Request	Scripture	Update/Answer Date

Date	Request	Scripture	Update/Answer Date

Date	Request	Scripture	Update/Answer Date

Date	Request	Scripture	Update/Answer Date

Date	Request	Scripture	Update/Answer Date

Date	Request	Scripture	Update/Answer Date

Date	Request	Scripture	Update/Answer Date

friday

worship God for His righteousness

I will ascribe righteousness to my Maker and I will give thanks to You, Lord, according to Your righteousness. I will sing praise to Your name, O Lord Most High, and my tongue shall declare Your righteousness and Your praise all day long. (From Job 36:3; Psalms 7:17; 35:28)

Your throne, O God, is forever and ever; a scepter of righteousness is the scepter of Your kingdom. You will judge the world in righteousness and the peoples in Your faithfulness. Your righteousness endures forever. It is everlasting. Your law is truth. Let my tongue sing of Your word, for all Your testimonies and commandments are righteous forever. (From Psalms 45:6; 96:13; 111:3; 119:142,172,144)

You are the holy God who shows Himself holy in righteousness. Only in You, Lord, are righteousness and strength. Your righteousness is near and shall not wane. O God, who is like You? Righteousness and justice are the foundation of Your throne and lovingkindness and truth go before You. Your righteousness will cause truth to spring up before all nations. Men shall eagerly utter the memory of Your abundant goodness, and shall shout joyfully of Your righteousness. (From Isaiah 5:16; 45:24; 51:5,6; Psalms 71:19; 89:14; 85:11; 145:7)

You restore my soul; You guide me in the paths of righteousness for Your name's sake and You have wrapped me with a robe of righteousness. Praise Your holy name. (From Psalm 23:3; Isaiah 61:10)

See also Psalms 11:7; 36:6; 65:5; 71:15,16; 85:11-13; 89:16; 98:2; 103:6; Hosea 2:19.

prayer for Christian impact in media and society

Pray for greater Christian impact in mass media and cultural or social services (Proverbs 1:7; Colossians 2:8; 3:17).

Local and other newspapers	Movies
Magazines	Community services
Television	Scientific research
Radio	Medical services
Commentators	

Pray:

- That publishers, producers, sponsors and performers will be awakened to God's principles and will recognize man's philosophy as empty deception.
- For the public to crave righteousness to be portrayed in the entertainment field (Matthew 5:6).
- That influential individuals in these fields will meet Christ and become ambassadors of reconciliation (II Corinthians 5:18-20).
- For God to impress upon your mind a list of personalities for whom He wishes you to pray.

Other requests:

Date	Request	Scripture	Update/Answer Date

Date	Request	Scripture	Update/Answer Date

Date	Request	Scripture	Update/Answer Date

Date	Request	Scripture	Update/Answer Date

Date	Request	Scripture	Update/Answer Date

Date	Request	Scripture	Update/Answer Date

saturday

worship God for His faithfulness and provision

"It is good to give thanks to the Lord, and to sing praises to Thy name, O Most High; to declare Thy lovingkindness in the morning, and Thy faithfulness by night" (Psalm 92:1,2).

"Know therefore that the Lord your God, He is God, the faithful God..." (Deuteronomy 7:9).

"If we are faithless, He remains faithful; for He cannot deny Himself" (II Timothy 2:13).

O Lord God of hosts, who is like You, O mighty Lord? Your faithfulness also surrounds You. Your lovingkindness, O Lord, extends to the heavens. Your faithfulness reaches to the skies. Your lovingkindnesses never cease, for Your compassions never fail. They are new every morning. Great is Your faithfulness. (From Psalms 89:8; 36:5; Lamentations 3:22,23)

Father, You have commanded Your testimonies in righteousness and exceeding faithfulness. You, who promise, are faithful. You have called me into fellowship with Your Son, Jesus Christ my Lord, and You will bring Your promises to pass. If I suffer according to Your will, I can entrust my soul to my faithful creator in doing what is right. (From Psalm 119:138; Hebrews 10:23; I Thessalonians 5:24; I Peter 4:19)

O Lord, who hears prayer, to You all men come. How blessed is the one whom You choose and bring near to You to dwell in Your courts! We will be satisfied with the goodness of Your house, Your holy temple. You are the trust of all the ends of the earth. You visit the earth and greatly enrich it. Blessed are You, Lord, who daily bears our burden. We praise You, O God, that You are to us a God of deliverance. Your eyes move to and fro throughout the earth in order that You may strongly support those whose heart is completely Yours. (From Psalms 65:2,4,5,9; 68:19,20; II Chronicles 16:9)

See also Psalms 23,27,36,37,65,68.

prayer for fellow believers

Pray for each other: for all fellow believers

Pray:
- For purification of our thoughts and deeds – that we may be fit instruments and channels of God's love (Psalm 139:23,24)
- That Christians might encourage and stimulate one another to love and good deeds (Hebrews 10:24).
- For individual needs: spiritual, physical and material (Philippians 4:6,7,19).
- That each may stand perfect and fully assured in all of the will of God (Colossians 4:12).
- For fellow believers' maturity and consistency in their personal Christian lives (Ephesians 3:14-20; Philippians 1:9-11; Colossians 1:9-12).

Other requests:

Date	Request	Scripture	Update/Answer Date

Date	Request	Scripture	Update/Answer Date

Date	Request	Scripture	Update/Answer Date

Date	Request	Scripture	Update/Answer Date

Date	Request	Scripture	Update/Answer Date

Date	Request	Scripture	Update/Answer Date

urgent requests

This section is included for quick access to urgent requests, upcoming events, temporary needs, other prayer lists, etc.

Use the monthly *Praise and Prayer Reminder* to augment this section if you receive it.

Date	Request	Scripture	Update/Answer Date

Date	Request	Scripture	Update/Answer Date

Date	Request	Scripture	Update/Answer Date

Date	Request	Scripture	Update/Answer Date

Date	Request	Scripture	Update/Answer Date

Date	Request	Scripture	Update/Answer Date

Date	Request	Scripture	Update/Answer Date

Date	Request	Scripture	Update/Answer Date

prayer for the evangelization of the world

"And Jesus came up and spoke to them, saying, 'All authority has been given to Me in heaven and on earth. Go therefore and make disciples of all the nations, baptizing them in the name of the Father and the Son and the Holy Spirit, teaching them to observe all that I commanded you; and lo, I am with you always, even to the end of the age'" (Matthew 28:18-20).

"Go into all the world and preach the gospel to all creation" (Mark 16:15).

"And seeing the multitudes, He felt compassion for them, because they were distressed and downcast like sheep without a shepherd. Then He said to His disciples, 'The harvest is plentiful, but the workers are few. Therefore beseech the Lord of the harvest to send out workers into His harvest'" (Matthew 9:36-38).

"...For My house will be called a house of prayer for all the peoples" (Isaiah 56:7).

Include praying for the nations and peoples of the world sometime during each week – daily, or on one particular day.

For example, if you will take just two minutes of each hour during a 15-hour day, naming 14 nations and their needs, you can pray for all 210 nations and protectorates in the world in one day!

- Pray for all in authority, believers, non-believers, missions, the persecuted, the suffering, etc.
- Pray for manpower, resources and opportunity to translate, produce and distribute the gospel among the 2.5 billion unreached peoples of the world.

- Pray for the penetration of the gospel into all areas of the world where there is not yet freedom to proclaim the gospel without hindrance.

specific world prayer

Not everyone can "go into all the world" personally. However, every Christian can have worldwide influence through effectual prayer.

Become a world changer through prayer. Use the enclosed map and list of nations to pray specifically for each country of the world. Work out a systematic approach, such as praying for 30 nations a day. This will enable you to pray for every nation once a week. Or pray for seven nations a day, a method which takes you around the world in 30 days. Or, you may want to pray by name for every nation every day.

Adopt a continent or a nation as a special prayer target, collecting as much information as you can which will enable you to pray intelligently. Knowledge of the historical, social, economic, cultural and religious conditions, which you may gain by reading about a country, will be helpful in understanding future prayer requests. You may want to go to a library to research the most up-to-date information available on your adopted country.

A recommended source for data:

World Handbook for the World Christian by Patrick Johnstone. William Carey Library, Publisher, 533 Hermosa Street, South Pasadena, CA 91303

This is a rich source of information about missions around the world for the prayer group leader and anyone who desires to pray in depth for world missions.

Date	Request	Scripture	Update/Answer Date

Date	Request	Scripture	Update/Answer Date

Date	Request	Scripture	Update/Answer Date

Date	Request	Scripture	Update/Answer Date

Date	Request	Scripture	Update/Answer Date

Date	Request	Scripture	Update/Answer Date

Date	Request	Scripture	Update/Answer Date

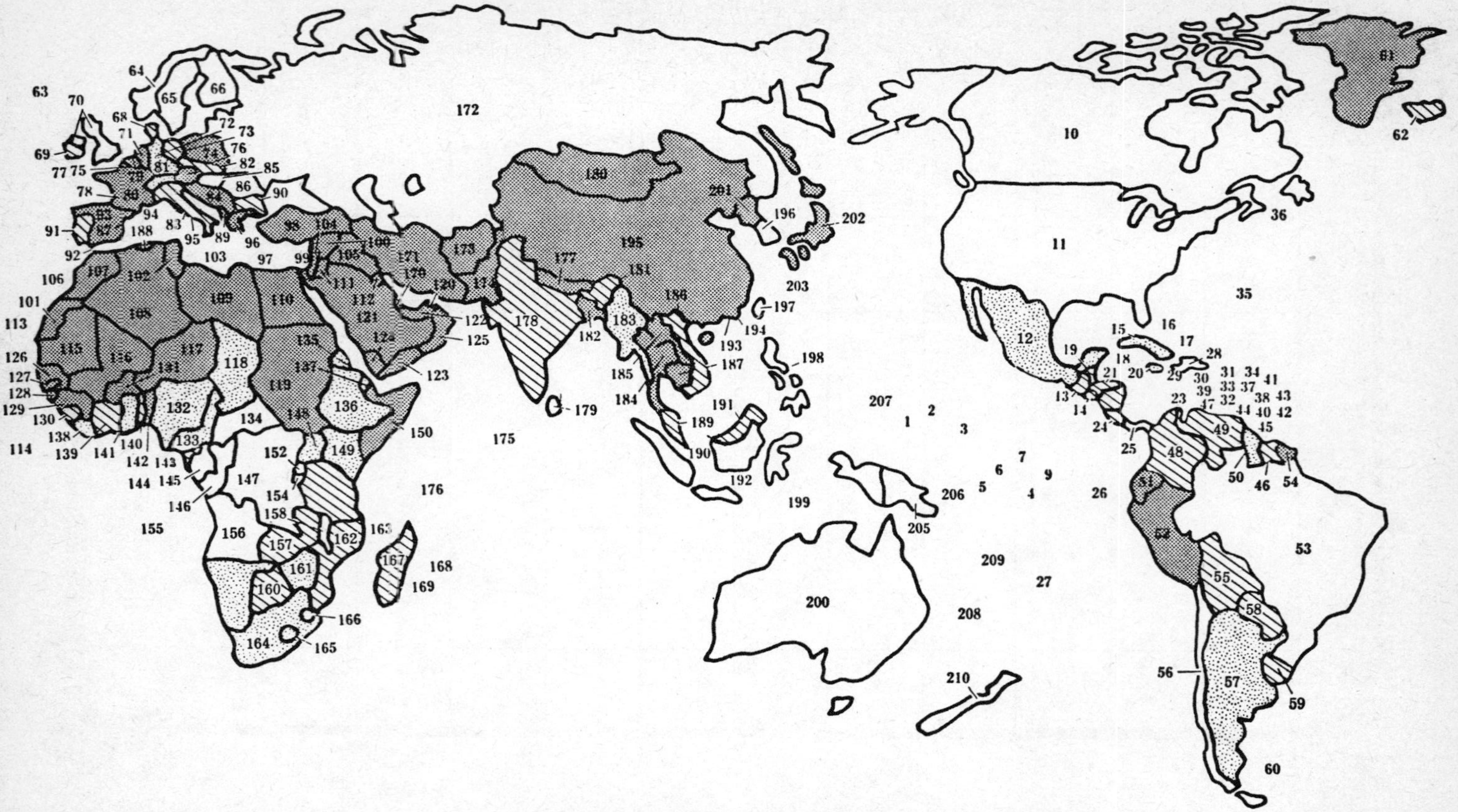

64
63
70
66
65
172
68
72
73
71
74
76
69
81
82
77
75
79
85
180
10
61
62
78
80
86
90
201
83
84
202
196
36
94
91
188
83
87
95
89
96
98
104
100
195
11
92
103
97
99
105
171
173
177
107
102
111
170
120
174
181
203
35
106
109
110
112
186
197
101
108
121
122
178
182
183
15
16
113
115
116
117
118
135
124
125
194
12
17
28
126
137
123
193
198
19
18
21
20
29
30
31
34
41
127
128
119
187
185
13
23
39
33
37
38
43
129
130
132
136
184
191
207
2
14
47
32
44
40
42
138
141
148
179
189
1
3
24
49
45
114
139
140
142
133
134
150
175
190
25
48
50
46
54
143
152
149
147
7
144
145
154
176
192
206
6
5
9
4
26
51
146
158
155
156
199
205
53
52
162
163
167
157
161
168
209
55
169
200
27
160
166
208
58
165
164
56
210
57
59
60

prayer for the nations

How To Use Your World Prayer Map

Plan A: Pray for seven nations each day. This will take you around the world each 30 days.

Plan B: Pray for 30 nations a day. This will enable you to pray for every nation once a week.

Plan C: "VISION BUILDER": Pray for 210 nations in one day; take two minutes to pray for 14 nations each hour for 15 hours. Just two minutes each hour spent in intercession on behalf of all in authority, believers, non-believers, missions, the persecuted, the suffering, etc., and have an impact for all of eternity.

What Do The Shades Mean?

The light shade [____] tells us that at the very least one out of 100 people in that nation is a believer in Jesus Christ. As you can see, both Russia and the United States are this light shade, meaning that not less than one in 100 in both countries are Christian. In actuality, one out of every three people in the United States is reportedly a born again believer, whereas it is estimated that one person in 13 is a Christian in the Soviet Union.

In the same manner, the [____] shade represents a range of one believer in every 100 to 200 people; [////] indicates one believer in every 200 to 500; and [____] means only one born again believer in every 500 to 1,000 or more people. In some of these countries the ratio is actually one believer in 5,000, or two one-hundredths of one percent!

KEY TO MAP - Countries Listed Numerically

AFRICA
101 Western Sahara
102 Tunisia
106 Ifni
107 Morocco
108 Algeria
109 Libya
110 Egypt
113 Canary Is.
114 Cape Verde Is.
115 Mauritania
116 Mali
117 Niger
118 Chad
119 Sudan
126 Senegal
127 Gambia
128 Guinea-Bissau
129 Guinea
130 Sierra Leone
131 Upper Volta
132 Nigeria
133 Cameroon
134 Central Africa Empire
136 Ethiopia
137 Republic of Djibouti
138 Liberia
139 Ivory Coast
140 Togo
141 Ghana
142 Benin
143 Rio Muni
144 Sao Tome and Principe
145 Gabon
146 Congo
147 Zaire
148 Uganda
149 Kenya
150 Somalia
151 Fernando Po
152 Rwanda
153 Tanzania
154 Burundi
155 Saint Helena
157 Zambia
158 Malawi
159 Namibia (S.W. Africa)
160 Botswana

161 Zimbabwe	201 North Korea	172 Union of Soviet Socialist Republics
162 Mozambique	202 Japan	
163 Comoro Is.	203 Okinawa	**NORTH AMERICA**
164 South Africa	**AUSTRALIA AND OCEANA**	10 Canada
165 Lesotho	1 Truk Is.	11 United States
166 Swaziland	2 Micronesia	12 Mexico
167 Madagascar	3 Kiribati & Tuvalu	13 Guatemala
168 Mauritius	4 Cook Is.	14 El Salvador
169 Reunion	5 Fiji	15 Cuba
176 Seychelles	6 Western Samoa	16 Bahamas
188 Spanish Morocco	7 Tonga	17 Turks & Caicos Is.
MIDDLE EAST	9 Fr. Polynesia	18 Cayman Is.
97 Cyprus	200 Australia	19 Belize
98 Turkey	205 Papua New Guinea	20 Jamaica
99 Lebanon	206 Solomon Is.	21 Honduras
100 Syria	207 Guam	22 Nicaragua
104 Israel	208 New Caledonia	23 Netherlands Antilles
105 Iraq	209 Vanuatu	24 Costa Rica
111 Jordan	210 New Zealand	25 Panama
112 Kuwait		28 Dominican Republic
120 Qatar	**EUROPE**	29 Haiti
121 Saudi Arabia	62 Iceland	30 Guadeloupe
122 United Arab Emirates	63 Faeroe Is.	31 Puerto Rico
123 South Yemen	64 Norway	32 Montserrat
124 Yemen	65 Sweden	33 British Virgin Is.
125 Muscat and Oman	66 Finland	34 Virgin Is.
170 Bahrain	68 Denmark	35 Bermuda
171 Iran	69 Ireland	37 Antigua
173 Afghanistan	70 United Kingdom	38 St. Kitt
174 Pakistan	71 Netherlands	39 Martinique
	72 West Germany	40 Trinidad
	73 East Germany	41 St. Lucia
ASIA	74 Poland	42 Barbados
175 Maldive Is.	75 Luxembourg	43 Dominica
177 Nepal	76 Czechoslovakia	44 St. Vincent
178 India	77 Channel Is.	45 Tobago
179 Sri Lanka	78 France	47 Grenada
180 Mongolia	79 Belgium	61 Greenland
181 Bhutan	80 Switzerland	
182 Bangladesh	81 Liechtenstein	**SOUTH AMERICA**
183 Burma	82 Austria	26 Galapagos Is.
184 Thailand	83 San Marino	27 Easter Is.
185 Laos	84 Yugoslavia	46 Surinam
186 Vietnam	85 Hungary	48 Colombia
187 Kampuchia	86 Romania	49 Venezuela
189 Malaysia	87 Andorra	50 Guyana
190 Singapore	88 Italy	51 Ecuador
191 Brunei	89 Albania	52 Peru
192 Indonesia	90 Bulgaria	53 Brazil
193 Macao	91 Portugal	54 Fr. Guiana
194 Hong Kong	92 Gibraltar	55 Bolivia
195 China	93 Spain	56 Chile
196 Korea	94 Monaco	57 Argentina
197 Taiwan	95 Vatican City	58 Paraguay
198 Philippines	96 Greece	59 Uruguay
199 Timor	103 Malta	60 Falkland Is.

KEY TO MAP - Countries Listed Alphabetically

173	Afghanistan	96	Greece	174	Pakistan
89	Albania	61	Greenland	25	Panama
08	Algeria	47	Grenada	204,205	Papua New Guinea
6	American Samoa	30	Guadeloupe	58	Paraguay
87	Andorra	207	Guam	52	Peru
156	Angola	13	Guatemala	198	Philippines
37	Antigua	129	Guinea	74	Poland
57	Argentina	128	Guinea-Bissau	91	Portugal
200	Australia	50	Guyana	31	Puerto Rico
82	Austria	29	Haiti	120	Qatar
16	Bahamas	21	Honduras	169	Reunion
170	Bahrain	194	Hong Kong	143	Rio Muni
182	Bangladesh	85	Hungary	86	Romania
42	Barbados	62	Iceland	152	Rwanda
79	Belgium	106	Ifni	155	St. Helena
19	Belize	178	India	38	St. Kitt
142	Benin	192	Indonesia	41	St. Lucia
35	Bermuda	171	Iran	44	St. Vincent
181	Bhutan	105	Iraq	83	San Marino
55	Bolivia	69	Ireland	144	Sao Tome	Principe
160	Botswana	104	Israel	121	Saudi Arabia
53	Brazil	88	Italy	126	Senegal
33	British Virgin Is.	139	Ivory Coast	176	Seychelles
191	Brunei	20	Jamaica	130	Sierra Leone
90	Bulgaria	202	Japan	190	Singapore
183	Burma	111	Jordan	206	Solomon Is.
154	Burundi	187	Kampuchia	150	Somalia
133	Cameroon	149	Kenya	164	South Africa
10	Canada	3	Kiribati	123	South Yemen
113	Canary Is.	196	Korea, South	93	Spain
114	Cape Verde Is.	201	Korea, North	188	Spanish Morocco
18	Cayman Is.	112	Kuwait	178	Sri Lanka
134	Central African Empire	185	Laos	119	Sudan
118	Chad	99	Lebanon	46	Surinam
77	Channel Is.	165	Lesotho	166	Swaziland
56	Chile	138	Liberia	65	Sweden
195	China	109	Libya	80	Switzerland
48	Colombia	81	Liechtenstein	100	Syria
163	Comoro Is.	75	Luxembourg	197	Taiwan
146	Congo	193	Macao	153	Tanzania
4	Cook Is.	167	Madagascar	184	Thailand
24	Costa Rica	158	Malawi	199	Timor
15	Cuba	189	Malaysia	45	Tobago
97	Cyprus	175	Maldive Is.	140	Togo
76	Czechoslovakia	116	Mali	7	Tonga
68	Denmark	103	Malta	40	Trinidad
137	Djibouti	39	Martinique	1	Truk Is.
43	Dominica	115	Mauritania	102	Tunisia
28	Dominican Republic	168	Mauritius	98	Turkey
27	Easter Is.	12	Mexico	17	Turks & Caicos Is.
51	Ecuador	2	Micronesia	3	Tuvalu
110	Egypt	94	Monaco	148	Uganda
14	El Salvador	180	Mongolia	122	United Arab Emirates
6	Ethiopia	32	Montserrat	70	United Kingdom
63	Faeroe Is.	107	Morocco	11	United States
60	Falkland Is.	162	Mozambique	172	Union of Soviet Socialist Republics
151	Fernando Po	125	Muscat and Oman		
5	Fiji	159	Namibia (S.W. Africa) Nauru	131	Upper Volta
66	Finland			59	Uruguay
78	France	177	Nepal	209	Vanuatu
54	Fr. Guiana	71	Netherlands	95	Vatican City
9	Fr. Polynesia	23	Netherlands Antilles	49	Venezuela
145	Gabon	208	New Caledonia	186	Vietnam
26	Galapagos Is.	210	New Zealand	34	Virgin Is.
127	Gambia	22	Nicaragua	101	Western Sahara
73	Germany, East	117	Niger	8	Western Samoa
72	Germany, West	132	Nigeria	124	Yemen
141	Ghana	64	Norway	84	Yugoslavia
92	Gibraltar	203	Okinawa	147	Zaire
				161	Zimbabwe

prayer for the president

There are 10 very definite areas which must be considered when praying for the President. "Lord Jesus, bless the President" is not sufficient. We need to ask God to enable the man in the office of President to:

Realize his personal sinfulness and his daily need of the cleansing power of Jesus Christ.

Recognize his personal inadequacy for the task and therefore depend upon Almighty God for wisdom, knowledge, understanding and courage to carry out the task.

Reject all counsel that violates spiritual principles and then trust God to prove him right.

Resist the pressure of those who would have him violate his conscience.

Reverse the trends of socialism and humanism in our land, both of which dethrone God and deify man.

Ready himself to forsake his political career and his personal ambitions, if to do so would be in the interest of the nation.

Rely upon prayer and the Word of God as the source of his strength and key to his success.

Restore dignity, honor, trustworthiness and righteousness to the office of the presidency.

Remember to be a good example in his conduct to the fathers and sons of the land.

Remind himself daily that he will be accountable to Almighty God for his attitudes, actions and motives while serving as President.

Prayer does not include criticism, for poison and sweetness cannot come out of the same mouth at the same time.

From "Stand Up, America"
by Charles F. Stanley

how to pray for world leaders

Jack Hayford

"First of all then, I urge that entreaties and prayers, petitions and thanksgivings, be made on behalf of all men, for kings and all who are in authority, in order that we may live a tranquil and quiet life in all godliness and dignity." (I Timothy 2:1,2)

1. Be convinced that God has placed these leaders in their positions. As to whether they rule in evil or righteousness, they will give account, but it is God's sovereignty that has ordained their term of government nonetheless (Romans 13:1-4).

2. It is the believers' responsibility to pray for all governmental leaders. Our calling is not to pass judgement on their rule but to be obedient to God's Word, to enter into prayer with intercession that order and peace may exist in each land (I Timothy 2:1,2).

3. Such praying makes possible the rise of righteous rule in any land for God overrules in all things when intercessory prayer prevails (Psalm 75:7-10). Further, such praying paves the way for fruitful evangelism to take place in each nation (I Timothy 2:3,4).

4. Pray for a nation's leader to be taught by God that the Lord Almighty is the source of his rulership. Pray that humility will fill the hearts of kings who learn to fear God just as Nebuchadnezzar learned to praise God (Daniel 4:34,35).

5. Pray for a nation's leader to love his people more than he loves himself in that he will serve as a shepherd and not as a task master (Micah 6:8 & Jeremiah 23:4,5).

6. Pray for the family of each national leader. God is able to work wonders in the heart of any man in this practical dimension of his daily life. Rightly ordered authority begins in the home in family relationships. Pray for miracles in the households of

world leaders. "All the saints greet you, especially those of Ceasar's household." (Philippians 4:22)

7. Pray that servants of kings and presidents will be won to Christ. All through history God has used servants to reach top leaders with the gospel. Kings and presidents see their servants quite frequently, either as secretaries or people who clean their palaces or prepare their food. These servants can personally give a gospel booklet or leave after them an imprinted message of God's love.

– World Literature Crusade

great commission prayer crusade

training materials

Great Commission Prayer Crusade Prayer Handbook, Volume I (350397)

Prayer Strategy Manual, Volume II (350215)

Mediated Prayer Workshop Training Package (Slides, Tapes and Film)

Live prayer workshop "How to Pray" transparencies

Prayer workshop packets for use of participants in a Dynamics of Prayer workshop.

CHURCH PRAYER STRATEGY MATERIAL

Prayer Congress Preview Film

Church Prayer Strategy Films from 1976 Prayer Congress (choice of 30 – write for brochure)

Church Prayer Strategy Film Study Guide

Complete list of the names of the heads of state (heads of government) for 211 countries of the world with their birthdays. Why not send them an encouraging birthday greeting and pray for them at the same time?

> "The king's heart is like channels of water in the hand of the Lord; He turns it wherever He wishes" (Proverbs 21:1).

To order any of the above or for further information write:
Great Commission Prayer Crusade, Campus Crusade for Christ, Arrowhead Springs, San Bernardino, CA 92414.